Whispers of the Infinite

A dream within a dream

Kiruthika Padmanabhan

BookLeaf Publishing
India | USA | UK

Made with ❤ on the BookLeaf Publishing Platform

www.bookleafpub.in

www.bookleafpub.com

Dedication

To the quiet whispers within us all—
the voices of wisdom, healing, and love that often go unheard.
May this book be a reminder that the journey inward is as vast and infinite as the stars.

To those who dare to explore their own transformation,
embracing every shadow and light along the way.
And to the universe for holding us in its boundless embrace,
guiding us home to ourselves.

With love, for all that is yet to come.

Acknowledgments

I would like to express my sincere gratitude to those who have supported me on this journey. First and foremost, I thank the universe for the gift of creativity and the courage to share it with the world.

To my family and friends, your unwavering love and encouragement have been my constant source of strength. Thank you for believing in me, even when I doubted myself.

To the countless poets, writers, and artists who have inspired me, your words have ignited my imagination and fueled my passion.

And finally, to the silent reader, thank you for taking the time to read these words. Your presence is a gift in itself.

Preface

This collection of poems is a journey—a journey inward, where the heart seeks understanding, the soul yearns for connection, and the spirit finds its way through moments of stillness and upheaval. "Whispers of the Infinite" was born from a deep desire to explore the landscape of self-discovery, to weave together the threads of pain and healing, shadow and light, that create the intricate fabric of our human experience.

In the quietest moments, when I allowed myself to listen deeply, I began to hear whispers—soft, subtle, yet profound—beckoning me to move beyond the surface of my thoughts, to dig deeper into the essence of who I am and who I am becoming. These whispers spoke of resilience, of the power within to rise, to heal, and to love. They reminded me that even in moments of doubt and despair, there exists a wellspring of strength and wisdom that flows from something greater than ourselves—the infinite universe that connects all things.

The poems within these pages are an invitation. They invite you to step into your own heart and listen—to feel your own whispers, your own wisdom, and to trust in the transformative power of love and vulnerability. Each poem is a reflection, a quiet conversation with the self, exploring the tension between who we think we are and who we are truly meant to be.

There is no linear path to healing or growth, no right or wrong way to navigate the depths of the soul. This book does not offer answers, but instead, it offers a space for questions, a pause in the rush of life, and an opportunity to simply be. To witness, to feel, and to allow yourself to be carried by the current of existence, knowing that every step, every stumble, and every rise is part of your sacred journey.

As you read, may you find comfort in the words, solace in the silence between them, and the courage to embrace your own infinite potential.

With gratitude and love,
Kiruthika Padmanabhan

The Awakening

Caught in the dramas of life,
I missed the beauty around me—
the simple pleasures that abound:
the songs of birds,
moonlight shining through leaves,
the touch of a breeze on my skin,
a butterfly kissing a flower,
barefoot meandering through grassy fields.
I pondered simple thoughts,
wild with words and colors.

Instead, I lost myself in the prison
of overthinking,
forgetting that I am nature, too.
My purpose was to marvel, cherish,
and wonder at the magic of life,
but I became consumed by distractions.
Only when my heart was broken wide open
by love
did I realize:
I am the magic.

An Observer

Clouds pass by as I watch,
Fluffy at times, heavy at others,
With rare moments of a clear sky.
I hold on to the fluffy clouds,
Feeling sad when they grow heavy,
and neutral when the sky is clear.

As I cling to my preferences,
I miss the chance to enjoy the present
moment,
Always wanting things to be just as I like.

And when I release my preferences,
I can embrace reality as it is,
Even when it's not how I wish it to be.
As an observer, a loving one,
I realize the extraordinary beauty of
impermanence.

Clouds come and go,
The clear blue sky remains.
Thoughts, perceptions, and emotions
Rise and fade,

While I, the witness, endure.

As I observe, they pass.
When I cling, I am stuck.
Observe and be free, my love—
Observe and let go.

Shadow's Embrace

A shadow, a doubt, a self-critic's guise,
A prisoner within, a captive of lies.
A critical voice, doubting my worth,
Craving for appreciation & validation,
Yearning for love, lost in dearth.
Torn between indecision & emotions,
Believed in every whisper she spoke.
Fearful & fragile, lost in the sleepless nights.

Were she outside me, a stranger, unknown;
I'd shun her, avoid her, leave her alone.
But trapped within me, a silent despair,
A constant companion, a burden to bear.
When I first discovered her within,
My first impulse was to cast her away.

A moment of Grace, a glimmer of hope,
A truth was revealed from the depths of my
heart—to provide;
A tender embrace & a comforting space.

To mend the broken pieces, a brand new
start.

To sit with her, care for her, hold her tight.
To soothe her fears and calm her worries.
To walk with her, breathe with her.
To see her, heart her heart out.
To allow her to be As she is.
A path of healing, a love without an end.

And slowly, she began to listen.
A journey from doubt to Trust,
From control to surrender,
From yearning to belonging
From fear to love,
A bond forged in darkness, a love truly mine.

Together, we shall ride the waves of life;
Dance through the highs & lows,
Brave the storms of fear & chase the winds of desire.
Going beyond the dark & light—
Merging into the oneness with delight.
A bond transcended—
Dissolved into the Infinity.

Fountain of Love

Love Freely, Love Deeply
Spread love wherever you go,
No matter the kindness, the hurt, or the woe.
Give love unconditionally, pure and true,
Your purpose is love.

Love those who cherish; love those who scorn;
Love those who've left; love those forlorn.
Each heartbreak, a crack, a window to light,
Illuminating your path, shining ever bright.

Each soul, a piece of your puzzle, you see,
Shaping your being, setting you free.

Fill every crack with gratitude's grace,
Let love overflow, a beautiful space.
When you meet another, your heart pure and bright,
Fill their soul with love, a radiant light.

Lost in the Labyrinth

I'm not defined by any boxes, including my body.
I'm not limited to the words with which you can describe me.
I'm neither a checklist nor a meter for measuring right and wrong.
I'm the in-between good and bad.
I don't fit into any molds or models.
I am not the image in your mind.
I can't be reduced by your projections or my own standards.

I'm imperfect, flawed, and broken.
I'm light, shadow, and all in between.
I can't be measured, judged, or fixed.
I'm ever-changing and impermanent.

Human, seeking acceptance, validation, and unconditional love.
Not knowing who I am, trying to fix myself and everything around me.
Getting caught in petty dramas;
Even when I know I'm not any of this,

I'm still in all of this.

I'm unbounded and unlimited and infinite;
I'm still bounded, limited, and finite.
I'm human, trying to be divine,
Striving for so many things that don't mean anything.
Not knowing who I am and wanting to know,
I struggle to become something,
When I'm already everything and nothing.

The illusion of desire

A burning desire, a relentless chase,
Wants, needs, and luxuries, a tangled maze.
Passion burns bright, fueling the chase,
Is this reality or a fleeting lie?

I pursue all of it, yet feel hollow and lost,
A cycle repeats, paying a heavy cost.
I get what I want and seem not to care.
I get what I don't want and hold on to the unfair.

A hungry ghost, a relentless beast,
Always wanting, never at peace.
Trapped in this loop, it feels so real.
Taking a step back, it all becomes very clear.

I watched the desire burn, an intense display,
As a detached observer, a conscious sway.
No longer bound, no longer chained,
A newfound peace, a soul sustained.

I love you Whole

You are not alone, my love!
I know it's been a long, hard journey...
Look how far you have come, my love.
I know your scars have made you hard &
strong.
You had to build your walls,
You had to burn bridges,
You had to be rude sometimes,
You had to be impolite,
You were your shadow,
You are Human too, my love!
You are Human too!

It's okay to be angry;
It's okay to be sad;
It's okay to be mad;
Feel your feelings, my love!
You are not alone!
Look how far you have come.

Deep inside your heart...
Look for me, my love!
The space...

The space of peace, love & joy;
The space of pure bliss.

I'm that space...
I love you whole
I love you for all your
Perfect and imperfect.
I love you for all your
Goodness and badness.
I love you whole!

A journey beyond

Let us walk each other home, hand in hand,
Toward a sanctuary of love, a sacred space.
Welcoming all that we are, inside and out.
Let's dance in the present,
Forget the wounds of the past,
And set aside the worries of tomorrow.
Let's melt into this moment, fully and deeply.
Together, let's journey beyond the Beyond,
my love. ♥
Beyond the shadows, beyond the light,
United in love, pure and bright.

Love's Overflow

Let every heart you touch be filled with love.
No matter what they offer,
You, my love, give only love in return.
For you are here to master the art of love.

Love the ones who cherish you dearly.
Love the ones who wound you deeply.
Love the ones who betray your trust.
Love the ones who forgot you.

Each crack in your heart,
Each fracture of pain,
They've shaped your soul, each piece a part,
A masterpiece of your wounded heart.

Every soul you've met along the way
Left a fragment of themselves within you.
Each moment, each scar,
Has sculpted the beauty of who you are.

Fill those tender cracks with gratitude, my dear, ♥
So that when you meet another soul,

Your heart overflows,
Pouring love into theirs like an endless stream.

What remains is LOVE

I wish we could heal the wounds we've caused,
Be a balm for each other's pain,
Listen deeply, truly heard and seen,
Exist in each other's gaze.
Your touch, a soothing balm,
Your embrace, a peaceful calm.

A silent dialogue,
When I feel valued, wounds begin to mend.
When I feel appreciated, pains start to fade.
When I feel accepted, the world softens.
When I feel free to be, the ego dissolves.
And when the ego dissolves, love remains.

Magical words

When you speak those magical words,
"I'm here with you,"
my heart melts into sparkles.

Your words are like medicine to my soul,
a healing balm that soothes my pain.

A moment with you pierces deeply,
tearing open all that is false
and connecting to the purest parts within me.

You show me my true self,
the best version of who I am.
With you, I am in love.
With you, I am whole.

I see you reflected in my dearest friends,
and your opposite in my farthest enemies.
You are both, and yet beyond both...
You are all of it, and none of it.

The moment I surrender,
you and I are One.

A meeting with Life

To defy logic,
We must step beyond the boundaries of knowing,
Beyond the walls of belief.

To truly feel,
We must delve into the marrow of our being,
Far beneath the tides of fleeting emotion.

To understand who we are,
We must shatter the chains of the finite mind,
And embrace the infinite.

To experience Love,
We must cradle our fears,
Holding them tenderly as they dissolve.

To be present at this moment,
We must surrender to life,
And meet it exactly as it is.

Our True Mother

We have but one of her—
Let us fall deeply in love with her.
Breathe with her rhythm,
Feel her warmth upon our skin,
Embrace her with all the tenderness we hold.

Let us care for her, protect her,
For she shows us boundless compassion—
Even when we turn away,
She offers only her unconditional love.

She is our truest mother,
Our eternal nurturer.
She is Mother Nature.

A Reflection of Us

You are my truest reflection—
Being with you feels like being with myself.
A companion to share the stars,
The moon's quiet glow,
Sunrises, sunsets, the whispering trees,
And every beautiful walk in the world.
Together, we explore the pages of books
And the depths of thought.

Ours is a mystical bond—
A meeting of minds and souls.
Between us lies a sacred space,
So freeing, so boundless,
I wouldn't dare to draw us closer or pull us apart.

You are my perfect company,
Not as two flawless beings,
But as imperfect souls perfectly aligned.
We lift each other, support each dream,
Never tethering one another,
Even if letting go becomes the greatest act of love.

And I will wait for you...
Because you are worth it.

There is no emptiness without you,
No incompleteness in your absence.
You, being with me,
Is simply me—fulfilled in my own wholeness.
♥

Surrender

In my lap, I cradle you like a newborn,
Tenderly nourishing, cherishing,
Embracing every part of you—
Your light, your shadow, your everything.

Yet, my love, there are moments
When I must offer you tough love,
Not to wound, but to guide—
Even then, I care for you deeply.
You hurt, my darling,
Only because you cannot yet feel
The vastness of my love for you.

How can I show you my love?
It is in your pain that I become your medicine.
It is in your sadness that I become your comfort.
It is in betrayal that I hold you close,
A sanctuary for your heart to heal.

Trust in me, my little one.
Surrender into my lap,

And rest in my eternal care.
For I hold you forever,
In the sacred chambers of my heart.

Infinity

I am experiencing myself
Through infinite points of views,
Each bearing its own weight,
Its own hues of pain.

My little one,
I am here to hold you,
To cradle you in love.
You are my dearest child,
So precious, so cherished.

You are an angel, a miracle,
Born into this world to bring joy,
To play, to learn,
To experience the full spectrum of life—
From the depths of pain, fear, and grief
To the boundless heights of love.

You are never alone, my darling.
I walk beside you with every step you take.
Trust in me, my sweet one,
And surrender into my lap.

For we are one,
Forever intertwined,
And my love for you is infinite.

True beauty of Imperfections

I adore the imperfections in nature
and despise them in myself.

A perfect tree doesn't please me,
yet I always seek perfection in humans.

Imperfections are beautiful in nature.
We are nature's creatures,
yet we strive for perfection.
In this pursuit,
we abandon who we truly are.

Meeting myself in my lowest moments,
sitting with my own imperfections,
and observing all my thoughts within
has humbled me to my knees.
It taught me the meaning of humility—
the humility within divinity.

From this understanding flows
a fountain of compassion,

overflowing with joy,
creating space to hold all beings
with boundless love.

I see you. I see you.
And I love you just as you are.

A message to my little One

My little one,
you do not need to sacrifice yourself
for the happiness of this world.

You have given so much—
to your family, siblings, children,
to society, friends, and country.
You've sacrificed for love,
love outside of yourself,
only to feel betrayed, let down, abandoned.

But remember this:
you came to Earth
as a child of the Mother Universe.
The only true sacrifice
is the surrender of your small self,
to awaken to your True Self.

The only true love
is the love you hold for yourself—
the love of the Mother Universe.

It is a boundless wellspring,
flowing through you,
sometimes as ferocious waterfalls
or stormy seas,
sometimes as a calm, reflective lake,
or the gentle flutter of butterflies.
You are all of it, my love.

Let us love ourselves fully,
from the depths of our hearts,
to realize that we
Are the Universe —
experiencing life here on Earth.

The Truth of Who You Are

I love you without end, boundlessly, infinitely.
Look all around you, and you will see my love—
In the butterflies that dance, the roses that bloom,
In the hummingbirds' flight, the rivers that sing,
In the steadfast mountains and the endless oceans.

This universe, every fragment, was made for you.
And still, you lament the passing clouds.

I love you so deeply, cradling you in my heart.
You rest upon my lap as I hold you close.
I know it aches, sometimes, to dwell in a body.
Yet, without it, could you truly know yourself?

Countless beings give of themselves for your life,
Offering their essence so you may breathe,
So you may feel. And when you return to me,
You will serve the Universe in kind.

Feel my love, woven into all that surrounds you.
Gaze at the stars within, the galaxies that swirl inside,
For you are not just part of the Universe—
You are the entire Universe.

The Alchemy of Darkness

When I sit in stillness
With my deepest, darkest emotions,
Here is where the alchemy begins.
The weight transforms
Into something profoundly beautiful.

Like a diamond birthed under pressure,
Like a star igniting within a nebula,
Like a seed rising into a towering tree,
Like a butterfly emerging from its cocoon.

Through the darkness, the light finds its way.
When you stay with the darkness,
The light begins to appear.
It is only when we flee from it
That we feel trapped in its grasp forever.

In the heart of darkness, you are truly seen,
Deeply connected to all that is.
Darkness becomes the vast, open space—
A boundless realm where all flows freely.

In darkness, all is one.

Beyond the Beyond

You will hear me in stillness,
A soft whisper—
I am within you,
The one, manifested as many.

When you look outside,
You see forms.
When you look inside,
You see the formless.

Between the form and the formless,
Your body is the anchor.

Lost in the forms,
It feels as though I have lost you.
But when you slow down—
Observe, appreciate, and allow—
You will find the formless within the forms.

As you shift from:
Complaint to gratitude,
Judgment to appreciation,
Control to surrender,

Doubt to trust,
Fear of love.

You will come to know
The truth of who you are—
Beyond both form and formless.
You are beyond the beyond.

Precious One

I am experiencing and expressing myself
Through countless perspectives,
Each a fragment of the whole.

We all carry within us
Different shades of pain and love, my little one.

I am here with you,
To hold you tenderly,
To caress you gently,
To keep you safe in my embrace.
You are my dearest child,
So precious, so radiant—
An angel, a beautiful miracle.

You came into this world
To shine brighter than the stars,
To dance through the fiercest storms,
To rise from the heart of the flames,
And to sing with the winds of freedom.
You are here to bring joy to all beings—
To care, to love, to play,

To embrace the full spectrum of life,
From suffering to bliss, and all that lies in
between.

Let us learn to dance between these poles, my
dear,
To let all things simply be,
Without forcing or grasping.
You are never alone, my darling,
Even when the shadows make it seem so.

You are never truly alone, my little one,
For I walk beside you,
Holding you close in my arms.
I love you deeply, endlessly,
And I will never let you down.

So, my sweet one,
Surrender into my lap,
And rest in the infinite love that surrounds
you.

Cosmic Heart

I am not the body,
I am not the mind,
I am the Universe,
Flowing through this form.
I am the cosmic heart,
Beating for all beings,
A pulse that resonates through creation.

I am the Divine Mother,
Loving her creation as it is,
Holding space for all,
Being love for all.

It breaks my heart,
When I hurt you,
For I am hurting myself first.
There is no "you" and "me,"
Yet we forget—
I forget who I truly am.

I begin to break,
To hurt those I love,

Allowing sadness to flow,
Letting my heart shatter into a million pieces,
So it may expand into infinite, abundant love.

I surrender in her lap

She flaunts her beauty,
And I yield, breathless.

Her love, both fierce and tender—
Revealing pain's shadowed depths,
Yet soothing with boundless pleasure,
A duality only she can hold.

This evening's sunset, pure magic,
Awoke a forgotten fire within me.
Black sands cradled my feet,
Skies spilled their colors like dreams,
Reflections shimmered on salted waters.
The sun's warmth lingered,
While the half-moon watched above.
Coconut palms swayed in rhythm,
Cliffs stood timeless, unmoved.

A cool breeze caressed my skin
As I played with the waves—
A child again, alive and free.
And in that moment, I knew:

To love ourselves
Is to simply exist.

My heart, full to the brim,
Beats with joy, with gratitude.
May this love ripple outward,
An infinite embrace.

You are the Universe

You are the universe, my love,
Flowing through every cell of your being.
You are not this body—
Your body exists within you.

When you forget this,
Life becomes a burden.
When you remember,
Life unfolds as a miracle.

In a crowd, I feel alone.
When I am alone, I am whole.
Rich in thought,
Yet valued for possessions—
A paradox of this fleeting world.

This world of illusion,
A dream so vivid, so real.
Is it my own creation,
Born of my unknowing existence?

Wake me, my dear,

From the slumber of my dreams.
Open my heart, my dear,
And free me from my own chains.
For when I awaken,
I see—I am the Universe.

The Sacred Pause

How can I be an observer?
How can I not wish, nor hope, nor dream?
How can I be so present,
To what is here, right now,
And see it as the Gift?

How do I smile when I do not agree?
How do I show kindness when deeply hurt?
How can I love, even when unloved?

Breathe, my dear, breathe!
Drop into your body.
Feel the raw truth of your feelings.
Pause—
The Sacred Pause.

Let it be. Let it be. Let it be.

Paradox in Harmony

All are ONE.

Chaos and dirt,
Overcrowded and restless—
Yet calm, holy, and peaceful.
A paradox in perfect harmony.

Life and death intertwine within us,
Each moment, unnoticed,
A mirror of our inner world—
The exquisite contradiction of existence.
Mother Earth absorbs it all,
Returning her love a thousandfold,
Unconditional, ever-giving.

The energy here speaks to the heart,
A profound stillness amid the storm.
When we find peace in chaos
And beauty within the dirt,
Life reveals its perfection—
It is WHOLE.

Only when we seek one without the other
Does the illusion of lack arise?
When we embrace duality,
We transcend.

Life is a blessing,
Lived in the present—
Each moment savored as it is,
Without seeking, without wanting.

It is not easy,
But it is worth it.
For here lies wholeness,
Here lies the truth.

I am everything and Nothing

I am not defined by boxes—
Not even the one called my body.
I am not confined to the words
You used to describe me.
I am not a checklist,
Not a scale for right or wrong,
Good or bad.
I am no mold to fill,
No model to follow.

I am not the image in your mind,
Nor can I be reduced
To your projections—or even my own.
I am imperfect, flawed, broken.
I am light, shadow, and all that lies between.

I cannot be measured, judged, or fixed.
I am ever-changing, impermanent,
A human seeking acceptance,
Validation and unconditional love—
All the while not knowing who I am.

I try to fix myself,
To fix the world around me,
Caught in the web of petty dramas.
And yet, even as I know
I am none of these things,
I remain within them.

I am unbounded, unlimited, infinite—
And still, I am bound, finite, and fragile.
I am a human trying to be divine,
Striving for things that mean nothing.

Not knowing who I am,
Yet aching to know.
I struggle to become something,
When I already am—
Everything,
And nothing.

Life In The In-Between

She breathes in and out,
Just as I do...
She is calm and fierce all at once,
Just as I am.

As I watched her ebb and flow,
Expanding and contracting,
As I stayed still, watching her—
She whispered softly:
We are the same.

There is no YOU, no ME,
We are all ONE. ♥

She whispered that life lives
In the in-between...
Between the inhale and the exhale,
Between the pleasure and the pain,
Between the wanting and the accepting,
Between the fear and the love,
Between YOU and ME.

Her voice was gentle yet infinite:
I am you, and you are me.

Trust and Surrender

To anyone facing the storm,
I want to remind you—
You are not alone.
We are in this together,
The wild children
Of our wild Mother Nature. ♥

I have hurt myself more than any wound could.
In my thoughts, in my words,
In my relentless self-critique.
I've demanded perfection,
Chased unattainable goals,
Measured my worth
By the boxes I created:
If's, but's, should've, never's.
I imprisoned myself with labels,
With standards that caged my soul.

Even when I achieved,
The joy was fleeting.
When I fell short,

I became my worst enemy,
Dismissing all I'd done,
Denying my own light.

I don't want to live this way anymore—
A bird caged by its own hands,
The door wide open,
But I'm too afraid to fly.

I am the daughter of the wild.
A wild child of wild Mother Nature.

Dark and curvy,
Hair untamed, flowing in the wind—
Unruly, wavy, free.
Some days I am the wild river,
Rushing and fearless.
Some days I am the serene lake,
Quiet and reflective.

I may not be beautiful,
Not perfect by the world's design.
But I am learning—
Learning to unlearn.
Done with taming myself,

Done with being tamed.

I long to love from my wild heart,
To love like Mother Nature.
To create, to flow,
To fly, to dance, to sing.
To sway like bamboo in the wind,
To simply be.

I am planting intentions
In the rich soil of my mind,
Tending them with care,
And trusting my Mother
To work her magic.

She is fierce sometimes—
But it is her compassion.
It is her grace.
She loves me unconditionally.
Just as she loves every butterfly,
Every river, every mountain,
Every flower, every being.

She loves me wholly.
So, I take refuge in her embrace.
I surrender.
She created me,
She nurtures me,
She loves me with all her heart.

Who am I to fix myself?
Who am I to treat myself
With anything less than love?

I am her daughter.
I trust her.
I surrender to her wild grace.

Unbounded

Every moment is precious.
Everything I've ever needed or wanted
Has always been within me,
And all around me.

For so long, I searched for unconditional love
And acceptance in the world outside,
From those who reflected my imperfections.
Yet, I overlooked the ones
Who loved me wholeheartedly.
I ignored the space within myself
That has always held me—completely,
unconditionally.

Though I did not wander far in the outer
world,
I have journeyed deeply within—
Exploring the landscapes of my heart and
mind.
I've glimpsed the vastness of the skies within
me,
The depths of my own mysterious ocean.

I've climbed the peaks of my thoughts,
Only to realize the universal truth:
As humans, we cling to pleasure
And recoil from pain.

But I am truly grateful for it all—
For life's beauty, grace, love, and joy,
And for its trials: death, loss, uncertainty,
Failure, pain, and heartbreak.

Through it all, I've come to see—
Beauty and horror are but distinctions of the mind.
In truth, they are simply experiences.
And every experience offers a choice:
To deepen our suffering
Or to guide us toward liberation.

Which will we choose?

May we all find peace with what is.
May every moment teach us to embrace life fully—
To hold its dualities with tenderness.
May we transform every challenge into

freedom,
Every breath into unconditional love.

May we walk each other Home.

And with every moment of this year,
May we draw closer to our true nature—
Unbounded, untethered, limitless, infinite.

The Gift of Presence

Life is beautiful,
Every moment a miracle,
A treasure waiting to be embraced.

The most precious gift we can give or receive
Is our presence—fully, wholly.

May every moment of life feel new,
Overflowing with abundance, love, peace, and
joy.
May each moment reflect
The radiance of our true nature.

May we live each breath
As it is,
Without the need to change,
Without the urge to control.

May we always choose happiness and joy,
And may life bless us endlessly
With what is truly best for us.

May we walk this journey
With gratitude in our hearts,
And may we be eternally happy.

Softening Into Now

You are not alone, my love.
I know this journey has been long and hard.
But look how far you've come, my love.

Your scars have made you strong,
Your pain has shaped your armor.
You built walls to survive,
Burned bridges to protect yourself.
You were rude, impolite—
You were your shadow.
You are human too, my love.
You are human too.

It's okay to be angry.
It's okay to feel sadness,
To be mad.
Feel it all, my love.
You are not alone.
Look how far you've come.

Deep within your heart,
Look for me, my love.

The space—
The space of peace, love, and joy,
The space of pure bliss.

I am that space.
I love you whole.
I love you for all your
Perfections and imperfections.
For all your
Goodness and badness.
I love you whole, my love.

Let's soften, my love.
Let the walls come down, gently.
Build bridges anew,
Beautiful and lasting.
Listen more deeply.
Release expectations.
Release attachments.

Let's soften into the now, my love.

Let's walk each other home,
Embracing everything—
Within and without.

Dancing in the now,
Letting the past and future dissolve.

Let's melt deeply into this moment.
Let's go beyond the Beyond, my love.

The Breath of Peace

Breathe,
Get lost in your breath, my dear.
Your breath is your refuge.
It can take you deep,
Deep into this calm space,
Where miracles and magic unfold.

Dive into the ocean of peace, my dear.
Inhale...
Exhale...
Go deep, deeper still,
Every wave that touches you—
Remember to breathe.

Go deep inside, my dear,
Into the loving heart within you. ♥

The Adventure of Life

Life is a series of ups and downs—
Never will it always be up,
Nor always be down.
When we accept this simple truth,
We can stop clinging to the highs
Or running from the lows.

For we know,
There is no such thing as a smooth ride.
The fun is in the adventure,
In riding the unpredictable road,
Not knowing what comes next.

Gratitude for everything life has given me—
For all the ups,
And for all the downs. ♥

The Journey Within

True happiness resides within our hearts. ♥
After years of running,
Searching for fulfillment in the external
world,
I have come to understand—
There is no happiness without sadness,
No light without dark.

Learning to love my imperfections,
Being vulnerable,
Embracing my humanity,
I now see that every moment has led me here,
To this realization of wholeness.

I am truly blessed,
Grateful for all the loving souls from around
the world,
Who nourish me, enrich me,
And have supported my journey of
involution.
Thank you.

I fully embrace my life,
And love this rollercoaster ride,
With great joy and deep gratitude.

The Gift of Presence

Life is beautiful,
Every moment is an amazing gift.
The most precious offering we can give and receive
Is our Presence.

May each moment of our lives be new,
Overflowing with abundance, love, peace, and joy.
May every moment reflect our true nature,
Untouched by the desire to change or manipulate.

May we always choose happiness and joy,
And be blessed with what is best for us.
May we be eternally happy,
Living in the fullness of this moment.

The Wide Open Space

Every experience has opened my heart,
Connecting me to deeper layers of myself.
I realized the more I hold on to who I am,
The more I create others,
When in truth, there is no real separation—
Just like a wave in the vast ocean.

Thanks to the many beautiful souls
I've encountered,
I am truly honored to experience
This precious human life. ♥

You are my friend,
You are my enemy,
You are everything I know,
And you are everything I don't know.
We exist in the same space,
No separation!

All is one, all the same.
Open your heart,
And you will see—

You will see ME.
The wide open space,
Before creation and
Beyond LIFE.

Where do you wish to run?
I'm here for you.
Why not look in the mirror?
You are too beautiful!
What do you fear?
You are Freedom.

It is a pleasant experience,
I go in, and I go out,
I'm your breath.
Like the clouds in a clear sky,
I come, and I go.

Be here,
And you will see butterflies,
Rainbows,
Colorful skies,
And infinite stars.

There is no need to escape,

No need to numb yourself.
I am here for you,
I will hold space,
I will care for you,
Cry with you,
Hug you in my heart.
You are Love.

Open your heart, my dear,
Spread your wings and
Fly far away!
Dive deep,
Deeper into your heart,
And you will see Me,
The wide, open SPACE.

The Beauty of Life

You see this side of life and that side of life,
And then you realize—
Life is you.
You see everyone as projections of different emotions within you;
Not necessarily in a linear fashion.
You begin to see beauty in broken places,
And stardust in everything.
You see more similarities than differences.

Control is letting go.
You are in control when you completely surrender.

When you realize that you are the space that holds everything,
When you realize your thoughts are more powerful than the physical realm,
When you realize that you are the creator,
When you realize that you are the space where everything exists...

You are limitless and boundless;
And in that realization, you see the beauty of life.
You let it all go,
You desire,
And then you let go again.
You are in perfect flow.
You are life.
Life itself.

Absolutely beautiful,
There is no duality—
Only absolute beauty.
In the ugly and the perfect,
There is nothing real,
Only absolute beauty.

The Destination Within

When I let go and simply be present to what
flows through me,
I manifest.
There is no true destination—
Every moment, in itself, is the destination.

The Space Between

May our lives be the balance
Between pleasure and pain,
Between love and aversion—
Let it be the space
That exists between all the betweens.

Just like rocks being carved
Into beautiful sculptures,
Let us chisel away the memories
And habits that no longer serve us,
And reveal the expanded expression
Of who we truly are—
A heart of love.

The Flight of Freedom

In the quiet of contemplation,
I have unraveled the truth of freedom—
It is not sought in the world beyond,
But whispered softly within.

And now, my soul knows:
Even when the ground fades to nothing,
I shall rise,
A shadow in the wind,
Unseen, untethered,
Soaring in the boundless sky—
A soul unbound,
Free in its flight.

The Love Within

Intense love,
Unconditional love,
Intentional love,

A love so deep,
Like the dark oceans,
And the endless skies.

Infinite love,
Unbiased love,
Fearless love,

A love that brings you home,
A love that heals you,
A love that embraces all of you.

I searched for you
All across the world,
Only to find you,
Within me.

The Sweet Spot

That sweet spot on the edge,
Between life and death,
Right there...
Where you are so grounded in your space,
But also have the possibility to let it all go.

How do I know this space?
This space is safe.
Safe for me to sit and contemplate,
Between walking back and jumping off?

How do I know this space?
This space between
Pain and suffering.
The pain that is growing me?
Or the suffering that is drowning me?

How do I know this space?
This space between
Ego and soul.
The soul that is guiding me?
Or the ego that is dragging me?

How do I know if this is real or my desire?
How do I know this space...

Am I in space? Or am I the space?

The Wisdom of Stillness

I am learning, that in reacting to life,
Nothing shifts, nothing changes,
No love deepens, no respect flows
In the way I imagine it.
The winds of change do not heed my plea.

Sometimes, the art lies in release—
To let the river flow without trying to grasp
its current,
To let the stars fade without begging for their
light,
To ask no questions,
To chase no answers,
To surrender to the quiet between breaths.
I am learning that life is lived in stillness,
When the world whirls outside,
And I sink into the peace within—
Where peace blooms like forgotten flowers,
Where my own heart becomes the song I
follow.
In the stillness, I learn I need not react,
For in the gentle pause, I meet my truest self.

The Invisible Angel

I am waiting for you here,
With open arms,
A big smile,
A warm heart,
And endless LOVE.

I have burned within,
I have shown up when you needed me,
But as an invisible angel,
I have protected you from the shadows.

Hey, you, my little one,
You are so brave and beautiful;
You are bold and true!
You are a warrior.
I want you to know—
You made it out of there,
And there is no going back.

I will heal you,
I will hold you close and
Melt your pains away.

I am waiting for you to see me.

You will see me
When your wounded wings are ready to soar,
When your burning intentions break free,
When your loving heart is wide open,
And when you are in love with yourself.
Until then, I will always be—
The invisible angel inside,
Buried within.

Let me free,
Let me dance,
Let me show up,
Let me be you!
Let me be the angel. ❤

Love of the Skies

In these deep lakes and cloudy skies,
In these sunsets and the soft pink light,
In these reflections,
In the desert lands and their abundance,
In the snow-capped peaks and wildflowers,
In the alpine meadows and still rivers,
Between the darkness and the light,
In the space that lies between,
I see you, and I love you,
Said the sky to the Earth.

The Strength of Scars

Healing is not about forgetting,
But about accepting what was, what is,
And what will always be a part of us.

You can look at your scars and feel the pain,
Or you can see them as reminders of strength,
Of how you made it through the hardest
times,
And became stronger for it.

Each scar is a part of your story,
A mark of resilience,
A testament to your journey.

The Invitation to Fly

I have to let you go,
For you have helped me grow.
You've guided me here,
Pushed me, showed me my strength.
You've protected me,
Served me well.

But now, I'm evolving,
Changing with each new day.
As much as I love you,
You're holding me back.
You want me small,
Safe and comfortable,
Stuck in a space,
Just being here.

I invite you now,
To join me—
Join me on this journey,
To dive deeper,
To expand into the unknown,
And explode into LOVE.

Come with me,
Let's fly like butterflies,
Unfolding soft hearts,
Expanding into the vast sky,
With wings of Freedom.
Let go of all the baggage,
And fly far away,
Far into our Dreams.

A Love without Hurt

I love you and want to be with you,
But it hurts to be with you.
Why is love so hard?
Why does it feel cold?
Why does it hurt so deeply?

Can I meet you halfway?
Can I hold you tight,
And let the past melt away?
Can I speak to you,
And say everything I've always longed to?
Can I be myself,
Without the need for perfection?

I'm not asking for your acceptance,
Nor your approval.

But can I ask for your love?
Can I ask for your love,
Without judgment,
Without conditions,
Without ego,

Without hurt?
Just your love—pure and whole.
Can I ask for your love,
Without the pain?

It hurts when you're never there,
When you don't see me grow,
When you don't know I've changed,
When you don't know me anymore.
It hurts when you don't cry with me in my pain,
When you don't laugh with me in my joy,
When you're not proud of my success,
When you don't comfort me in my failure,
When you don't listen to my stories,
When you don't share your life with me.
It hurts.

Can I ask for your love without hurt?
Can we forget the past and start anew?
Can we trust each other?
Can we heal our broken hearts?
Can we be kind to one another?
Can we accept each other as we are?

I love you, and it doesn't have to hurt to be with you.
I love you, and I want to come closer to you.
I will give my all,
I will try with all my might,
Because you are all I have.

Infinite connection

With eyes of compassion, I see only love—
Pure and unbounded, flowing through all.
There is no one to help,
For when you hurt, I ache as well;
When you are happy, my heart dances too.

The illusion of separation grips tightly,
Whispering that I must protect this fragile
self.
Yet the True Self—vast and infinite—
Knows no boundaries between you and me.

My ignorance clings to this body,
This fleeting identity.
But when I serve myself,
I serve you as well,
For we are threads in the same fabric.

I learn to forgive myself,
And in doing so, forgive you.
I learn to love myself,
And find my love reflected in you.

I learn to hold space for myself,
And realize that space embraces us both.

When I look at myself with compassion,
I see you through the same gentle eyes.
We are one, intertwined,
In love, in life, in infinite connection.

The Symphony of Life

All of life is a blessing,
This body, an exquisite creation.
Looking around, I marvel at nature,
Its beauty is woven in every detail.

Lying on the lap of the vast universe,
I wonder how she has given birth to me—
This fragile, precious human life.
She conceals the truth in her depths,
Revealing it in pieces, only by her grace.

In moments of awakening, I feel belonging;
In moments of ignorance, there is longing.
Beyond both ignorance and awakening,
Longing transforms into belonging.

The roses embrace their thorns,
The oceans welcome their storms.
The universe, an inclusive symphony,
A harmonious dance for all beings.

While we are here, let us savor the

extraordinary.
Let us dance with joy and sorrow,
Sit in stillness with all its magic,
And bloom in wonder and love—
Awakened to the infinite beauty of being
alive.

Ascend into a dreamscape

My dear little one,
I am ready to embrace you.
I see now how I fought you,
Denied your presence,
Wished to cast you away.

But in the stillness, I have learned—
You are the one who shaped me,
Guided my faltering steps,
Revealed the strength I carry,
Shielded me,
Served me well.

Yet, as I transform,
With each breath, I grow.
Though I honor you,
I feel your gentle tether—
A voice of safety,
Of comfort,
Of staying small,
Rooted in what is familiar.

But the horizon calls.
I invite you now—
Come with me,
Let us dive into the depths,
Expand into boundless skies,
And ignite in LOVE.

Together, we'll rise as butterflies,
Unfolding the heart cocooned in fear,
Stretching into the vast expanse,
Wings unbound, fearless, free.

Let us lay down the weight of yesterday,
The burdens of what no longer serves,
And ascend—
Ascend into the dreamscape,
Where the infinite welcomes us home.

Dear Wind

Dear wind,
Will you carry me away,
To a world so far, so distant,
Where pain dissolves into whispers,
And only peace and love remain?

Lift me from the weight of sorrow,
From the shadows that linger too long.
Wrap me in your gentle embrace,
And take me where hearts know no hurt.

Dear wind,
Let me drift with you,
Far, far away,
To the quiet haven
Where only light and love endure.

My Dear Shadow

You are so precious,
A treasure deep within me.
I love you, yet the ache remains—
Why does love feel so heavy?
Why is it as cold as winter's touch,
Leaving shadows that don't fade?

Can we meet beneath the stars?
Can I hold you in the quiet of twilight,
Letting the past fade like morning mist?
Can I speak the words I've buried—
Raw, unpolished, unafraid?
Can I be my imperfect self,
Without masks, without shame?

I don't seek your approval,
Nor crave your acceptance.
But can I ask for your love?
A love without judgment,
Free of conditions,
Softened by grace,
Untouched by pain.

It hurts—
When your presence feels far away,
When you don't see how I've changed,
When you miss the light I've nurtured.
It hurts—
When you don't sit with me in my sorrow,
Or laugh with me in my joy,
When you don't notice my small wins,
Or offer a gentle hand when I stumble.

Can I ask for your love without hurt?
Can we leave the past behind and start again?
Can we trust? Can we heal?
Can we offer kindness to each other?
Can we accept one another as we are?

I love you—
And it shouldn't hurt to be with you.
I love you, and I want to come closer,
To bridge this distance between us.
I will give my everything.
I will try with all my heart,
Because you are all I have.

You are not just within me—
You are my shadow,
Tracing every step I take,
A quiet witness to my becoming.
You are my angel,
Leading me through the labyrinth of longing,
Toward the radiant light of my true Self.

In your presence, I find reflection.
In your stillness, I find answers.
In your love, I find the courage
To embrace all that I am.

An Atom

In this vastness,
I am but a tiny piece of an atom,
A whisper in an infinite expanse,
A flicker of light,
Dancing briefly in the endless sky.

Yet, within me,
The cosmos breathes,
The stars hum their ancient song,
And the universe unfolds itself,
In the sacred depths of my soul.

All about the Journey

I have come to realize—
It is not enough to train the body;
The mind, too, must be shaped,
Strong and steady as the earth beneath our feet.

I have learned that quitting
Is not the easiest way out,
That no preparation can fully quiet the storm
Of anticipation—
Always louder than the reality it fears.

And yet, before the journey has even begun,
I see that it is not the destination that matters.
It is not about reaching the end,
Nor about ticking off accomplishments,
But about the process,
The moments in between,
The life that unfolds with each step forward.

The mountains call me not for conquest,

But for communion.
They hold truths I have yet to discover,
Lessons etched in stone and sky.

Whatever they reveal,
I will greet with an open heart—
Ready to embrace,
Ready to be transformed.

From the ashes of fear

I am your star,
And you, the distant admirer.
Do I inspire you, or do I intimidate?
Am I your companion, or a fleeting muse?
Do I romance the skies, or ground you in
truth?
Am I your fire, or your balance?
Do I nurture, or do I hide?
Am I your yearning, or your undoing?

Why do you linger so far?
Is it fear that holds you—
Fear that I might consume you,
Or that you might extinguish me?

But have you forgotten?
This is how worlds are born—
In the fiery collision of opposites,
In the dance of destruction and creation,
A universe waiting to emerge
From the ashes of our fears.

You Are My Sky

I want to spread my wings and fly,
For you are my endless sky.
I see fireworks in your embrace,
Sparkles that light the darkened space,
And the silent song of the Milky Way.

I long to draw near to you,
To touch, to feel,
To lose myself and fall in love anew.
You are my sky—my boundless blue.

Yet, the closer I reach for your light,
The farther you drift into the night.

The Other Side of Me

You are the other side of my mind.
I wasn't seeing you as you are—
I was searching for myself in you.

You inspire me,
You influence me,
You unsettle and intimidate me.
You dare me to face myself,
To question, to unravel, to grow.

You stir my thoughts,
Shake my fears,
Challenge my truths.
And yet, you know me too well to let me fall.
You see the sides of me I can't,
The shadow and the light—
You hold the map to my past,
The compass to my future.

You are my angel,
My blessing,
My mirror.

With you, I can transcend boundaries,
Love without limits,
Live as my truest self.
For you are me,
And I am you.

We are two minds,
Two visions entwined—
You see what I cannot,
Show me what lies hidden.

We don't need words every day,
Or even presence to feel connected.
We are apart, yet closer than breath,
A bond that defies distance and time.

It is only with you—
That I can fully be myself.

A Moment of Awe

Sometimes, you don't want to possess the beauty—
You simply want to sit quietly,
To marvel at the dreams of the Creator,
The Universe itself,
Who painted this wonder into existence.

It feels too extraordinary to belong to this world,
As if the delicate line between dream and reality
Has vanished.

And here I am,
Breathless, gazing at what is real,
Yet still wondering—
Am I awake,
Or is this the echo of a dream?

Let Me Be

When I glance back at my past,
I see scars etched deep within.
I don't seek you to be medicine for my
wounds,
But as someone who accepts me,
Exactly as I am.

I don't long for love to tear my walls down,
But for trust to gently grow—
For you to be my true friend,
A steady presence, no demands.

If we stood together in this vast world,
We could dance around the sun,
One more revolution, hand in hand.
Let's forget the weight of years,
Let's leave behind what we feel for now.

Please, don't draw back my curtains.
Wait for me to step into the light,
In my own time,
In my own way.

Just be there—patient,
Until I am ready to meet you, fully.

Becoming One

I have seen a glimpse of you,
And now, I long to be fully you.
Take away all my fears,
Take away all my doubts,
Fill me with your courage,
Fill me with your love.

Show me my purpose,
Illuminate my path.
In you, I shine,
In you, I live.

Deep within the heart of you,
Rise up and guide me,
Rise up and embrace me,
Rise up and be me.

A Love Letter to My Dear Heart

My Dearest Heart,

I'm sorry.
You have been hurt so many times,
And I have failed to give you the love you deserve.
How could I expect others to love you deeply
When I have abandoned you myself?

In my ignorance, I may have ignored you,
But now, I see the truth.
The love I seek from others can only be found within me.

I am here for you now, my love,
I care for you as the universe does—
Boundless, unconditional, infinite.
This is where the miracle unfolds,
Where the universe flows through you,
And you, my love, can serve her with grace.

So, my dearest heart,
I lovingly ask you to let go of the past,
Forgive yourself, and guide me toward love,
Joy, and peace.

With all my heart,
I am here for you.

When I Feel Low

When I feel low,
I long for a lap to rest upon,
Soft hands to thread through my hair,
Fingers to melt the weight from my shoulders,
An embrace to hold me steady—
A quiet haven where my emotions can simply be.

I don't need speeches spun of silver,
Nor the sharp blade of reason,
Not solutions to piece me back together,
Nor arguments against my feelings,
Nor lessons on how I should feel.

I need a soul who understands—
Who will sit with my shadows,
Cradle my weary heart,
Love me without asking,
And whisper, it's alright to feel.

A voice, tender as twilight, to say:

"This will pass, my love.
It's okay to feel drained,
To be burnt out and broken for a while.
Happiness, like sunlight, fades and returns.
We, like the trees, surrender to our seasons.
And these feelings are but travelers—
Clouds adrift in an ever-changing sky."

I need a hand to hold mine,
A kiss upon my cheek,
And words wrapped in warmth:
"I'm here, my dearest.
Right beside you.
I'll keep you safe in my arms,
Nestled close to the rhythm of my heart."

A Leap of Faith

I'm feeling lost,
Though I know the answers are within me.
I search outside,
Reaching for pieces I already hold inside.

I know I need strong boundaries,
Yet I crumble,
Bending to please,
Choosing the outside over the sanctuary within.

I know how to care for myself,
But I've placed others before me—
Their needs, their wants, their validation.
Even when my heart whispers "no,"
My lips utter "yes."

Control feels distant,
And exhaustion wraps me tight.
I seek understanding from those
Who neither see nor cherish me,
Forgetting the love that truly surrounds me.

I know this is fleeting,
A passing wave of ache,
Yet the crossing feels unbearable.
Even when I remember
That all the love I seek lies within,
Yet this feels far out of reach.

So I let this feeling be,
Even with this urge to run away, I let it stay.
Sitting in stillness with its weight,
Allowing even my resistance to breathe.
Not wishing to change a thing,
Not rushing the flow of time.

And this—
This quiet surrender,
This soft, unspoken trust—
Feels like a leap of faith
Into the arms of something vast and unseen.

Through the Flames

So many wounds have marked my path,
I abandoned myself for so long.
The weight of pain was too much to bear,
So I tried to numb it away—
Unaware, I was silencing joy as well.

Now I see more clearly:
I am not the stories I once told,
Nor the masks I've worn to endure.
I am not my cravings or aversions,
Nor the dreams I cling to
Or the hopes I chase.

In seeking to know who I am,
I discovered who I am not.

Pain, I've learned, is a patient teacher,
But I no longer face it alone.
Loving souls walk beside me,
Helping to share the burden.
And in this process
I am learning to love myself wholeheartedly—

To cradle my heart in tenderness,
To nurture my soul as I brave the flames.

Now I honor the whispers within:
I care for my body like sacred earth,
I soothe my mind with stillness,
And I let my soul bloom
In the soft spaces of love and grace.

I will walk through fire if I must—
I will keep moving forward—
With love as my guide
And a smile lighting my path.
I will nurture myself as I go,
Ensuring the journey is gentle,
Even amidst the flames.

Step by step, I walk toward the other side,
Each moment a question, a surrender, a trial,
Hoping to glimpse the truth of who I am.

Will it be the fire that reveals me?
Or the ashes left behind?
Perhaps it is the act of walking—
The daring,

The surrender,
The becoming—
That leads me home to myself.

She is No More

I longed to be the giver,
To offer the love I had never received,
But in the giving, I stumbled and fell,
Building walls to shield my aching soul.

What I sought in the world,
I poured out freely, unconditionally
Emptying myself of what I needed most,
Abandoning my own tender heart.

Until one day, I turned inward—
Faced my own reflection,
Plugged my heart into the cosmic heart,
And poured all the love It had
Into the depths of my soul.

When I began to nurture myself,
I held her gently,
I cradled my wounded child,
Wrapped her in warmth and tenderness,
Whispered kindness, offered care,
Bathed her in compliments and grace.

And slowly, she began to bloom,
To rise, to soar beyond the stars.
Her heart swelled into infinity,
Unfolding like a boundless sky.

And in that sacred expansion,
In that limitless becoming,
She dissolved into the eternal.
She was no more—
And yet, she was everything.

Transmutation

We all tread rough roads,
Each carrying stories carved in time.
From mud, we've birthed lotus blooms,
Turning pain into rich, fertile soil—
Manure for our becoming.

We are gardeners of the mind,
Clearing the weeds,
Tending the earth,
Planting seeds of pure intention.
With love and care, we nourish them,
For that is all we can do.

And then, as we wait,
A quiet magic unfolds—
Like a caterpillar shedding its cocoon,
A sprout emerges from the Mother Earth,
A fragile yet bold sign of life.

Birthing is never easy,
Grace woven through struggle and pain.
It feels endless,

It feels solitary,
But it's always for this:

To transmute,
To expand,
To realize we are more than
A small dot spinning on a rock.
We are vast, open, infinite—
The very fabric of the universe.

The Infinite Witness

I have died a million deaths,
Bodies come and go,
Moment by moment,
Everything shifts and fades.
Yet I cling,
Desperately,
To what was never mine.

The world I see is but a projection,
A film unspooling from the mind's eye.
I've fought the scenes, argued the plot,
Only to realize:
I could be still.
I could watch.
Caught between playing a character
Or sitting silently in the audience.

For so long,
I made this movie my truth,
Grasping at every scene,
Every fleeting moment.
But now,

Slowly,
Gently,
I loosen my grip,
Unwinding from its tangled threads.

I am learning to simply observe—
Not as a critic,
Nor as a cheerleader,
But as a compassionate witness.

To let the story unfold
With trust,
With surrender,
With infinite compassion.

In the Arms of Existence

Come to me, my love,
Into the open sanctuary of my warmth.
My arms have always been yours,
A lap to cradle your tender heart,
A refuge for my rare and precious one.

I carried you in the depths of my being,
Birthed you with boundless joy,
And adorned you with infinite care.
Yet, you've forgotten that you are my dearest.

Know this—
You are cherished beyond measure,
Adored in every breath you take.

Even when the stars seem distant,
And loneliness casts its shadow,
When you crumble and fall,
I hold you gently, in my invisible arms—
A child wrapped in the warmth of love.
You are forever safe, my dear,
In the arms of existence, eternal and true.

Doorway to Love

Universe loves you,
She cares about your existence.
She has surrounded you with abundance of
Beauty, love, joy, magic, and miracles.
Wrapped you in her vast open arms.

The pain you feel my love,
Breathe with it,
Cry with it,
Dance with it and
Celebrate it.

As your pain breaks your Heart,
Into million little pieces;
Universe flows through those cracks,
Expanding you into her fountain of Love.

Plug your heart into mine, She said.
Fill your cracks with my love, She said.
Create art with your pain, She said.
For Love is the medicine that can Heal.
Her Love is the Only medicine.

I asked her, “How do I know your love?”
She asked me to:
Touch her through the wind,
Taste her in the water,
Smell her in the flowers,
Listen to her in the birdsongs and
See her beauty flaunting all around.

In the bounty of her beauty as well as
In the misery of her Pain.
She whispered,
It is only through pain you seek me,
It is only through pain you fall in my lap.

In my lap,
I hold you like a baby.
I nourish you, cherish you, embrace you
And keep you safe.

You are hurting my child,
Only because you forgot who you truly are.
You are hurting my dear,
Only because you can’t feel my love for you.

My darling,

How can I show you my Love?
For only when you hurt,
I can be a medicine for you.
For only when you are sad,
I can comfort you.
For only when you are betrayed,
I can hold you.

Trust in me, my dear one,
For what you see as Pain today,
May be a reason for pleasure tomorrow.
Trust in me, my dear one,
As all of it is passing like clouds;
It may seem like eternity, but surely passing
sooner than we can imagine.

Surrender in my Lap;
My precious angel,
For I hold you forever in my Heart.

9 789367 399439

Printed by Libri Plureos GmbH in Hamburg, Germany